My Healthy Body

BLOOD
AND HEART

Jen Green

ALADDIN/WATTS
LONDON • SYDNEY

© Aladdin Books Ltd 2003

Produced by:
Aladdin Books Ltd
28 Percy Street
London W1T 2BZ

ISBN 0–7496–5110–5

First published in Great Britain in
2003 by:
Franklin Watts
96 Leonard Street
London
EC2A 4XD

Editor:
Katie Harker

Designer:
Flick, Book Design & Graphics
Simon Morse

Illustrators:
Aziz A. Khan, Simon Morse,
Rob Shone, Ian Thompson

Certain illustrations have
appeared in earlier books
created by Aladdin Books.

Printed in UAE
All rights reserved

A CIP catalogue record for
this book is available from the
British Library.

Medical editor:
Dr Hilary Pinnock

Dr Pinnock is a GP working in
Whitstable, Kent. She has written and
consulted on a wide variety of medical
publications for all ages.

Contents

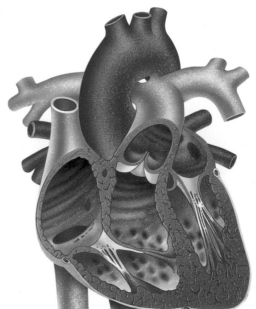

Introduction

Did you know that the warm, red sticky stuff that oozes out when you cut yourself is actually your body's lifeline? Blood carries oxygen and nourishment around your body, and also removes harmful waste. Your heart is a tireless pump that sends blood flowing around your body 24 hours a day, throughout your life. This book tells you all you need to know about your circulatory system and how to keep it in good shape for a healthy body.

Medical topics

Use the red boxes to find out about different medical conditions and the effects that they can have on the human body.

You and your blood

Use the green boxes to find out how you can help improve your general health and keep your circulatory system in tiptop condition.

The yellow section

Find out how the insides of your body work by following the illustrations on yellow backgrounds.

Health facts and health tips

Look for the yellow boxes to find out more about the different parts of your body and how they work. These boxes also give you tips on how to keep yourself really healthy.

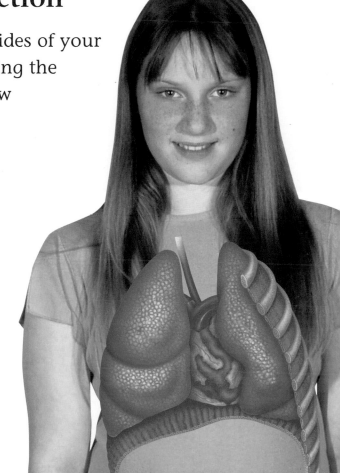

Your circulatory system

Your blood, heart, and a network of fine tubes called blood vessels make up your circulatory system. Like a river that never runs dry, blood flows ceaselessly around your body, collecting waste and delivering oxygen and energy to all body parts that need them. Humans and most animals have red blood, but some have blue, brown or clear blood. Lobsters (right) have blue blood.

Your heart beats about once a second every minute of your life, pumping blood around your body. Exercise helps to keep your heart fit and well.

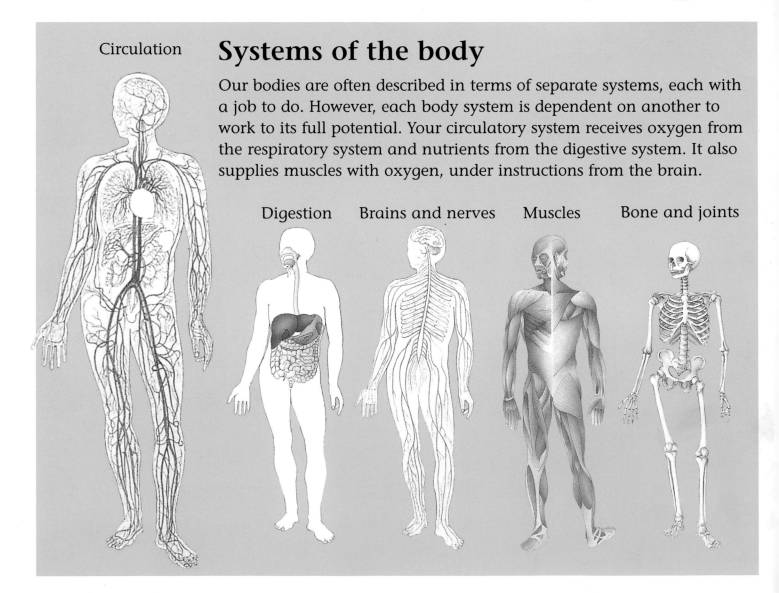

Circulation

Systems of the body

Our bodies are often described in terms of separate systems, each with a job to do. However, each body system is dependent on another to work to its full potential. Your circulatory system receives oxygen from the respiratory system and nutrients from the digestive system. It also supplies muscles with oxygen, under instructions from the brain.

Digestion   Brains and nerves   Muscles   Bone and joints

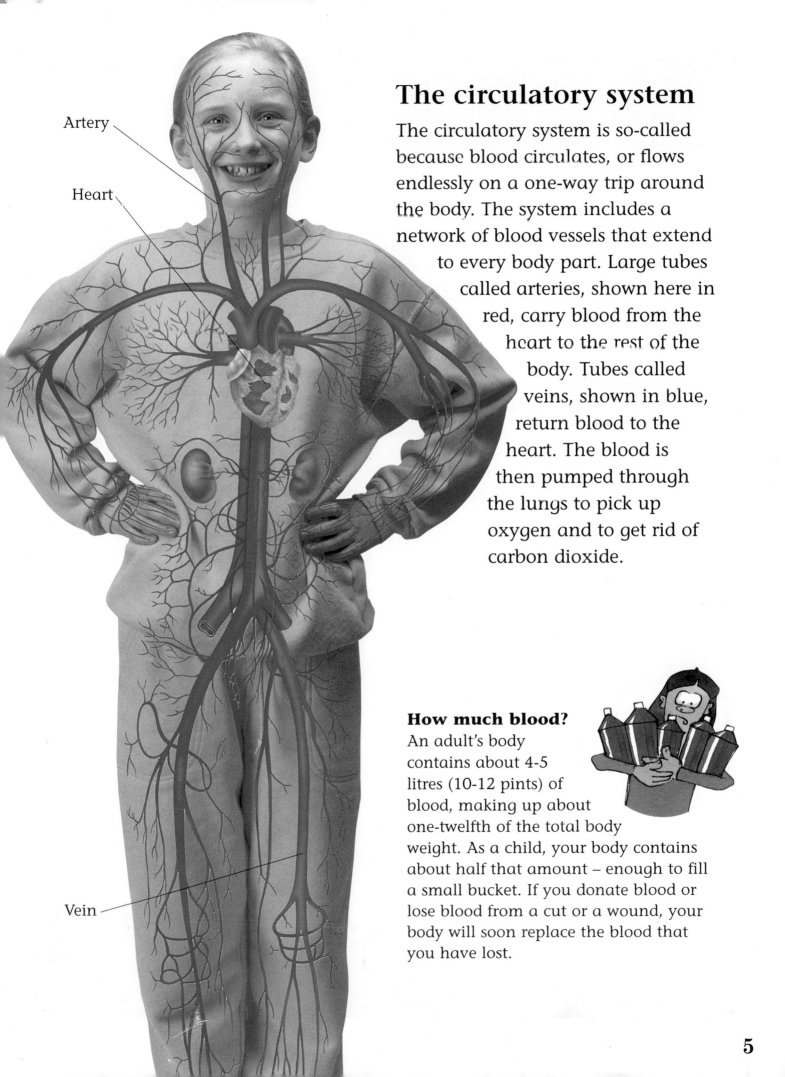

Artery

Heart

Vein

The circulatory system

The circulatory system is so-called because blood circulates, or flows endlessly on a one-way trip around the body. The system includes a network of blood vessels that extend to every body part. Large tubes called arteries, shown here in red, carry blood from the heart to the rest of the body. Tubes called veins, shown in blue, return blood to the heart. The blood is then pumped through the lungs to pick up oxygen and to get rid of carbon dioxide.

How much blood?
An adult's body contains about 4-5 litres (10-12 pints) of blood, making up about one-twelfth of the total body weight. As a child, your body contains about half that amount – enough to fill a small bucket. If you donate blood or lose blood from a cut or a wound, your body will soon replace the blood that you have lost.

What is blood for?

Your blood does so many different jobs and is vital to your health. Blood supplies all the tissues of your body with a continuous supply of oxygen and nourishment to keep them working. Blood also removes waste, which would otherwise build up and poison you. Blood distributes warmth around your body, transports chemicals (called hormones) that help coordinate body functions, and constantly fights infection.

Your blood acts as a delivery and waste collection service rolled into one. The service operates continuously, 24 hours a day, seven days a week!

Transport system

Blood is your body's main transport network. It carries oxygen, and also energy-rich sugars, vitamins and nutrients to all body parts that need these supplies to do their work. As cells and organs work, they produce waste, including carbon dioxide gas. Blood carries this gas away to the lungs so you can breathe it out. It also delivers other waste to the liver and kidneys to be destroyed or filtered out.

Hormones

Hormones are your body's chemical messengers, controlling processes such as growth and development. They are produced by glands around your body and released into the blood to travel around the circulatory system.

6

Fighting infection

Special white cells in your blood helps to defeat germs and other harmful substances that make you ill. They engulf harmful bacteria and viruses, and disable or destroy them. Extra white blood cells can also be quickly made if they are needed. If viruses multiply faster than your body can defend itself, you will become ill. Stress, a poor diet and lack of sleep can leave you more vulnerable to infection.

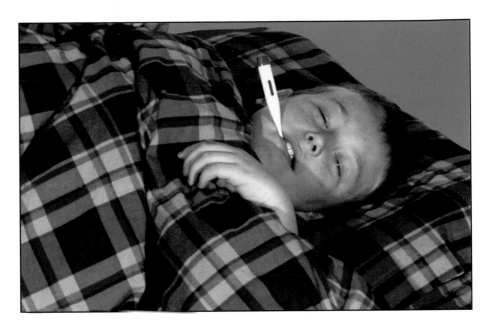

Keeping circulation healthy

Regular exercise helps to keep your circulatory system healthy. Strenuous exercise such as running or swimming strengthens heart muscles. A varied diet also helps to keep your heart, blood and circulatory system working well.

Transporting warmth

Like the water in a central heating system, blood spreads warmth evenly throughout your body. It redistributes heat from busy parts such as the heart and liver to cooler parts such as resting muscles. This helps to regulate your body temperature, keeping you at an even, and healthy, 37°C.

What's in your blood?

A drop of blood the size of a pinhead contains five million red blood cells, 15,000 white blood cells and 250,000 platelets.

Your blood is made up of billions of cells, all floating in a watery liquid called plasma. Your blood contains three main types of cells, each with a different job to do. Red blood cells transport oxygen around your body and carry away waste carbon dioxide which is dissolved in the plasma. White blood cells fight various kinds of infection and platelets help your blood to clot.

Blood cells

Red blood cells are small and shaped like doughnuts. They are red because they contain a red, iron-rich chemical called haemoglobin. It is this substance that carries oxygen. White blood cells are larger than the red cells. They come in various shapes and sizes, designed to fight different germs. Platelets, which help blood to clot, are the smallest blood cells.

Anaemia

Anaemia is an illness that occurs when the blood does not have enough haemoglobin to carry oxygen. People with anaemia may feel faint, look pale (above) or feel tired all the time. Anaemia is often caused by a lack of iron in the blood, so it may be treated by taking iron tablets or by being given extra blood.

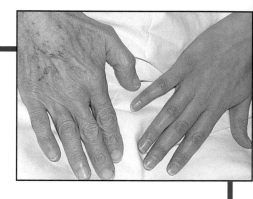

White blood cells

⊚ Blood groups

All human blood is not the same. There are four main blood groups, known as A, B, AB and O. Some types of blood cannot safely mix with others. Medical staff giving patients blood in hospital must be careful to supply blood of the right group, or the patient's body may react to it.

Parts of blood

The diagram shows the proportion of the different parts in your blood. Watery plasma makes up 54 per cent. Red blood cells make up almost all of the remaining 46 per cent, and give blood its colour. White blood cells and platelets together add up to just one per cent.

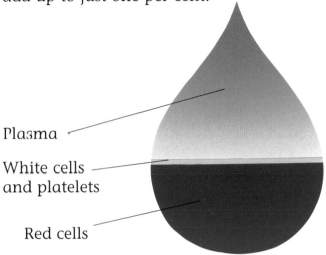

Plasma

White cells and platelets

Red cells

Plasma

Plasma is a yellowish liquid containing hundreds of different substances, including dissolved sugars, salts, minerals, hormones, proteins that are used to clot blood and medicines that you might have taken. Plasma transports these around the body to where they are needed. Patients suffering from certain illnesses may be given a transfusion of pure plasma.

Platelets

Red blood cells

How is blood made?

Most blood cells begin life in the spongy bone marrow inside certain bones, and then pass to other organs to finish developing. Blood cells don't last forever. When they die they are broken down by the liver to be used in the digestive process. Like the oil in a car engine, your blood is changed regularly to keep it in the very best condition.

Red blood cells live for about four months, platelets for just one or two weeks. White blood cells last from half a day to longer than a year, depending on the type.

Blood factory

Red blood cells are made in the jelly-like bone marrow inside the bones shown in red on the right. Other blood cells are also made in bone marrow. Special cells in the marrow divide to form new blood cells. These then pass to other organs to complete development.

Food for blood

Iron is essential to keep red blood cells healthy. It is needed for the red chemical, haemoglobin, that carries life-giving oxygen. Eating iron-rich foods such as eggs, red meat, and green vegetables like cabbage, helps to top up levels of iron in your blood.

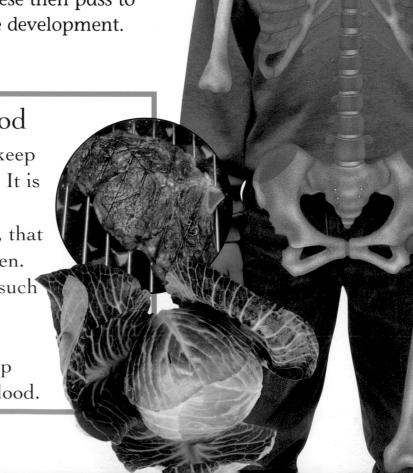

10

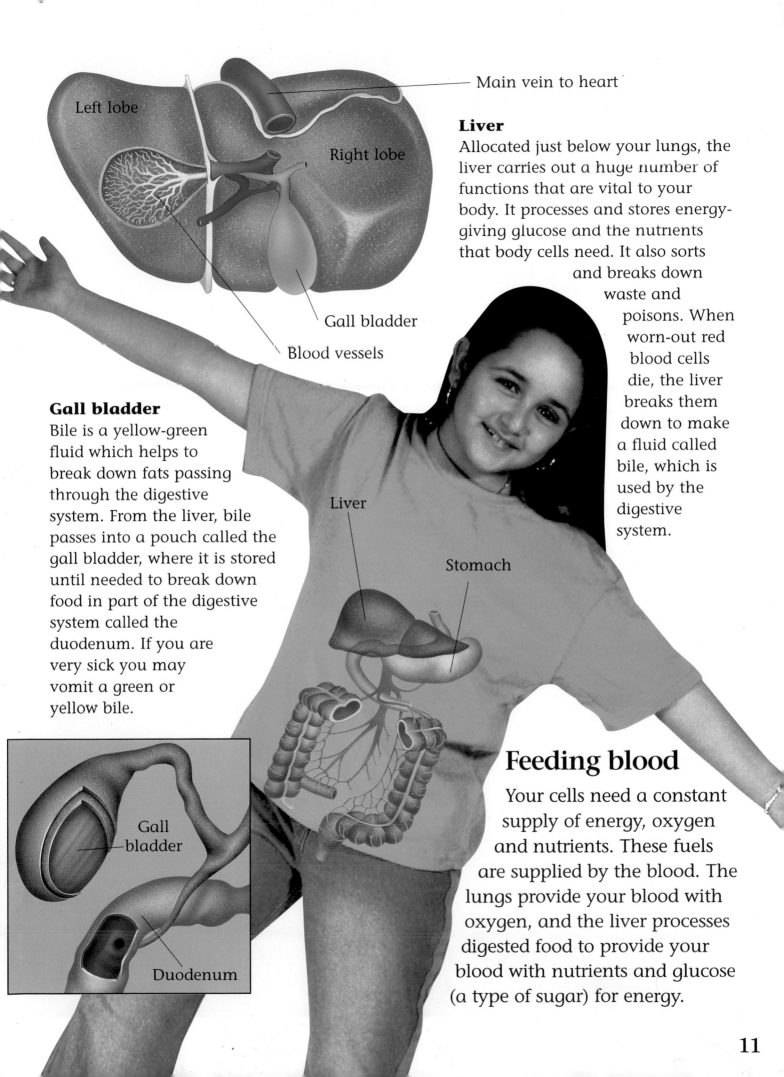

Left lobe

Main vein to heart

Right lobe

Gall bladder

Blood vessels

Liver

Allocated just below your lungs, the liver carries out a huge number of functions that are vital to your body. It processes and stores energy-giving glucose and the nutrients that body cells need. It also sorts and breaks down waste and poisons. When worn-out red blood cells die, the liver breaks them down to make a fluid called bile, which is used by the digestive system.

Gall bladder

Bile is a yellow-green fluid which helps to break down fats passing through the digestive system. From the liver, bile passes into a pouch called the gall bladder, where it is stored until needed to break down food in part of the digestive system called the duodenum. If you are very sick you may vomit a green or yellow bile.

Liver

Stomach

Gall bladder

Duodenum

Feeding blood

Your cells need a constant supply of energy, oxygen and nutrients. These fuels are supplied by the blood. The lungs provide your blood with oxygen, and the liver processes digested food to provide your blood with nutrients and glucose (a type of sugar) for energy.

Blood vessels

Your circulatory system consists of three main types of blood vessels: arteries, veins and capillaries. Arteries carry blood away from your heart and divide many times to form capillaries. In the capillaries, oxygen and nourishment seep through to body cells, in exchange for carbon dioxide and other waste. Capillaries carrying waste then join together again to form wider veins which return blood to your heart.

An adult human has about 96,000 km of blood vessels in total! If laid end to end they would circle the Earth more than twice.

Veins and arteries

The blood flowing through arteries, leading from the heart to the rest of the body, is bright-red in colour because is is rich in oxygen. Blood returning to the heart in veins is lower in oxygen and so purplish-red. Arteries and veins often run side by side. You can see veins through your skin, which look blue. Blood passing though your arteries flows at a higher pressure, surging more strongly than blood in your veins.

Capillaries

Both veins and arteries have watertight walls so blood flowing through them does not leak away. Capillaries have much thinner walls, through which oxygen and nourishment can pass to reach body cells.

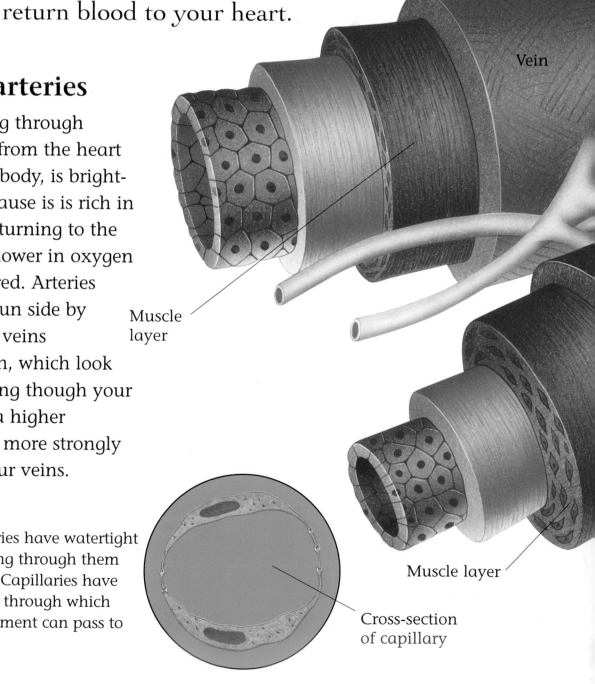

Vein

Muscle layer

Muscle layer

Cross-section of capillary

Smoking

Smoking damages the heart and circulatory system as well as organs such as the lungs. Poisonous chemicals in cigarette smoke reduce the ability of red blood cells to carry oxygen. Nicotine, the drug in tobacco, can cause extra heartbeats and palpitations. Tobacco also damages the linings of blood vessels that supply the heart and brain with oxygen.

Valves in vein to stop blood flowing the wrong way

Blood vessel walls

Arteries are wide, with thick, muscular walls that can stand up to the pressure of blood surging through them. Veins are also wide, but with thinner walls because blood returning to the heart surges less strongly. Capillaries have thin walls and are so narrow that blood cells pass along them in single file.

Artery

Vein   Artery

Fatty foods

Blood vessels can become clogged with fatty deposits from high-fat foods such as cheese, chips, cakes and biscuits. The fatty material builds up on the lining of blood vessels and hinders the flow of blood. Cutting down on fatty foods and eating plenty of fruit and vegetables daily can help to prevent these deposits building up.

Good and bad cholesterol.

Cholesterol is a fatty material (shown below) made by the liver from substances called saturated fats in food. Cholesterol plays a vital role in body cells, but too much cholesterol increases your risk of heart disease later in life. Reduce your cholesterol level by eating foods containing unsaturated fats instead of saturated fats, and cutting down on fatty foods generally.

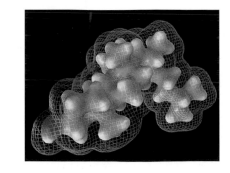

Your heart

Your heart is a hollow, muscular bag which beats about once a second, pumping blood around the circulatory system. The heart is actually two pumps, each powering a separate blood cycle. The right side pumps blood to your lungs to collect and return oxygen. The left side pumps oxygen-rich blood to the rest of your body.

Your hard-working heart pumps an average of 300 litres (600 pints) of blood every hour, day in, day out, all through your life.

The heart

The heart is broadly shaped like a cartoon drawing of a heart, except that the narrow part points sideways, not downwards. The heart has two sides – each with a small upper chamber called an atrium, and a larger lower chamber called a ventricle.

Left atrium

Left ventricle

Right atrium

Right ventricle

Love hearts?
All around the world, the heart is a common symbol of love and emotion. However, you feel love with your brain, not your heart. Your heart seems to skip when your feel scared or excited, but this happens under instruction from the brain.

Heart muscle
The heart is made of a special muscle, called cardiac muscle, that works constantly but never gets tired. Like all muscles, heart muscle needs oxygen to work. This is supplied by blood carried in coronary arteries.

14

Upper and lower chambers

Blood returning to the heart collects in the two atria. As your heart muscles relax, blood is squeezed from the atria into the ventricles. Powerful muscles in the ventricles then tighten to force blood from the heart. Valves between the atria and ventricles prevent the blood from flowing backwards.

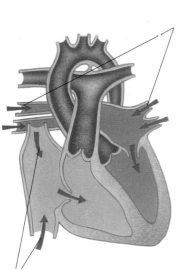

Heart valve closed

Blocked flow

The coronary arteries, which supply the heart with blood, can become partly blocked by fatty deposits. A painful condition called angina results when a narrowed artery hinders the flow of blood to the heart. If a narrowed artery is completely blocked, the person suffers a heart attack (see page 23).

Oxygenated blood from lungs enters the left atrium and is pushed through a valve into the left ventricle.

The left ventricle contracts and forces oxygenated blood into the body.

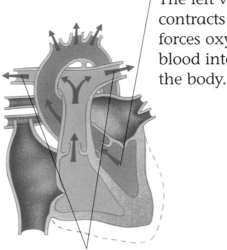

De-oxygenated blood from the body enters the right atrium and is pushed through a valve into the right ventricle.

The right ventricle contracts and forces de-oxygenated blood to the lungs.

Where is the heart?

Your heart lies between your lungs, at the front of your chest and slightly to the left. Both heart and lungs are protected by the bony rib cage. Your heart fits snugly inside its own chamber which allows it to beat freely. Your heart is about the same size as your fist.

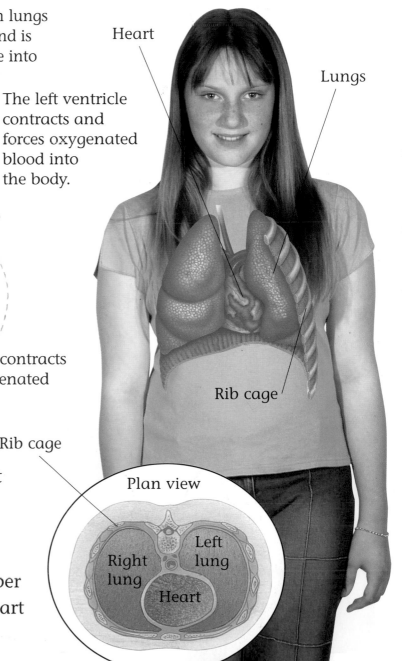

Heart

Lungs

Rib cage

Rib cage

Plan view

Right lung

Left lung

Heart

15

Heartbeat and pulse

About once a second, your heart muscles contract (tighten) and then relax again to pump blood around the body. The valves of the heart open and close to control the blood flow, creating the regular lub-dub sound of your heartbeat. Each beat sends a little bulge of blood called a pulse surging along your arteries. You can feel your pulse at various points in the body.

Small creatures have a much faster heartbeat than larger animals. A mouse's heart beats hundreds of times a minute, whist an elephant's heart beats around 20-25 times.

Find your pulse

You can feel the pulse most easily where arteries run over bones just under the skin, in places such as your neck, groin and ankle. Find the pulse in your radial artery by pressing two fingers on your wrist, just below the mound of your thumb. Don't use your thumb to feel for the pulse, as it has a strong pulse of its own.

Feel the bulge
Blood surges along your arteries to stretch the vessel walls and create a little bulge each time your heart beats (left). Use a stopwatch to count the number of beats in a minute to find out how fast your heart is pumping (shown right). This is called checking your pulse.

Seeing heartbeat

A machine called an electrocardiogram (ECG) (right) measures electrical activity in the heart and the action of heart muscles. Each peak shown on the screen represents one contraction of the ventricles. Doctors use these scanners in hospitals to check for heart problems.

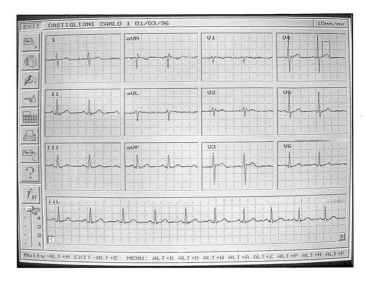

Blood pressure

Blood pressure – the force of the flow – is greatest as blood leaves the heart to surge along your arteries. The pressure gradually slackens as blood flows through the fine capillaries and the pressure is weakest along veins returning blood to the heart. Doctors and nurses can easily measure blood pressure in their surgery, using a simple device called a 'sphygmomanometer'.

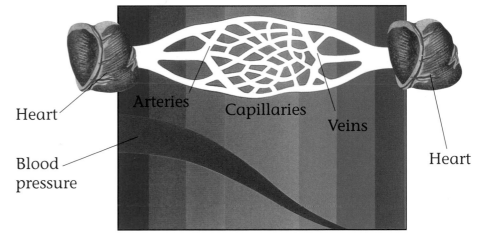

Heart

Arteries   Capillaries   Veins

Blood pressure

Heart

Aerobic exercise

Jogging, swimming, cycling and other moderately strenuous sports make your lungs and heart work harder to supply your muscles with oxygen. These are all forms of aerobic exercise, which is good for you because it strengthens your heart and lungs. The word aerobic means 'with oxygen'.

Cleaning the blood

Like speedy sprinters, blood cells take about a minute to make one circuit of your body, calling in at your lungs on the way.

As blood travels around your body, it collects various kinds of waste which must be removed by your lungs, kidneys and liver. In the lungs, blood gets rid of carbon dioxide, and picks up a fresh supply of oxygen. Your blood is filtered as it passes through the liver, and excess salts and minerals are filtered by the kidneys.

Oxygen passes from the blood to body cells.

Cardon dioxide passes from body cells to the blood.

Gas transfer

All body cells need oxygen to work properly. Oxygen comes from the lungs and is carried by the blood to your body cells. Cells also create waste, including carbon dioxide. This waste seeps through the thin walls of the capillaries to be transported by your blood into the lungs where it is breathed out.

Blood vessels

Airways

Respiration

In your lungs, your airways divide many times to end in microscopic air bubbles called alveoli. Oxygen-rich air passes through the walls of these little sacs to enter your bloodstream. At the same time carbon dioxide seeps through the opposite way, into the alveoli. You get rid of this waste gas by simply breathing out.

A mesh of fine blood vessels surrounds the alveoli (left). Each lung contains over 250 million of these miniature air sacs.

Drinking fluids

You lose about 2 litres (4 pints) of water each day as your kidneys filter blood to remove waste. All this fluid must be replaced by liquid from food and drink. Keep your body healthy by drinking plenty of water every day.

The urinary system

The urinary system filters blood to remove unwanted salts and minerals. Waste liquid is removed by the kidneys which lie just behind your stomach and liver. This liquid, called urine, passes down two tubes called ureters, to be stored in the bladder. When you go to the toilet, the waste travels down another tube, the urethra, to leave the body.

The kidneys

Your two kidneys filter blood to remove impurities. The outer layer of each kidney contains about a million tiny filtering units called nephrons. Waste removed by the nephrons trickles down channels into the centre of each kidney, and then flows down the ureters to the bladder, where it is stored before leaving the body.

Twin filters

Every day, all the blood in your body passes through your kidneys about 400 times. This means that the kidneys filter a total of about 2,000 litres (400 gallons) of blood a day.

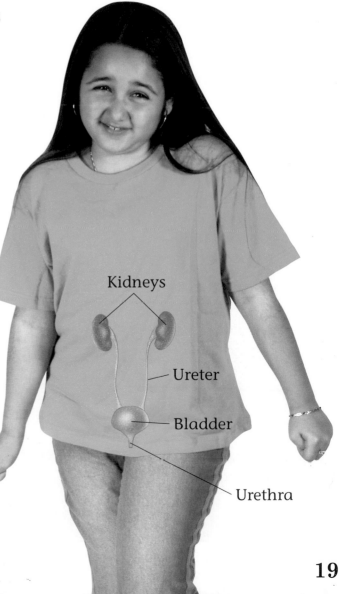

Kidneys

Ureter

Bladder

Urethra

Fighting infection

White blood cells play a key role in defeating germs and other 'outsiders' that invade your body. They constantly patrol the body to seek out and destroy germs and diseased cells. A milky-white fluid called lymph also circulates through the body, helping to beat infection.

White blood cells are your body's front-line troops in the battle against infection.

— Adenoids

— Tonsils

— Heart

Vaccination

Vaccination is a procedure which triggers the body's natural immune (protective) system. A weakened version of a disease is usually given by injection. This prepares the body to fight off more dangerous forms of the same disease.

Spleen —

Lymph nodule —

Bone marrow —

Lymph nodes in your neck, armpits and groin area contain white blood cells that destroy germs.

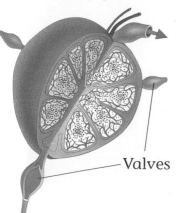

— Valves

Lymph system

The lymph system is a drainage system that removes excess fluid from cells and guards against infection. Lymph has its own circulatory system which uses valves to help it flow. Capillaries force out the pale liquid which bathes body cells, drains through the lymph network and re-enters the blood. The tonsils, adenoid glands and lumps of lymph tissue called 'nodes', are all part of this system.

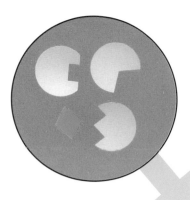

1. The many different kinds of white blood cells are designed to recognise different germs and other invaders.

2. When the right white blood cell comes upon the germ, it attaches to it. The blood cell and germ fit together like a key in a lock.

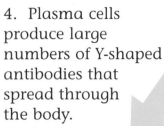

3. The white blood cells then multiply and change into special cells called plasma cells.

4. Plasma cells produce large numbers of Y-shaped antibodies that spread through the body.

5. The antibodies seek out and destroy the invaders, defeating the infection.

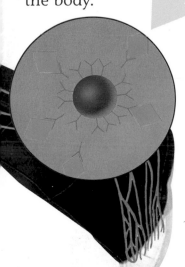

The immune system

White blood cells are always on the lookout for 'germs' like bacteria and viruses. Germs carry chemicals called antigens on their surface. White blood cells recognise antigens and respond by making chemicals called antibodies. These antibodies latch onto antigens and neutralise or destroy them.

Raised temperature

When germs get into your blood they can cause an infection. Your temperature may rise as your immune system works overtime. If the infection is in your throat, the lymph nodes or 'glands' in your neck may swell and feel tender, as the blood cells in your glands work to make you better.

Leukaemia

In an illness called leukaemia, certain white blood cells become cancerous and multiply very quickly. This means that they are no longer able to do their work of fighting infection. Leukaemia is a serious illness, but it may be treated using drugs or through a bone marrow transplant.

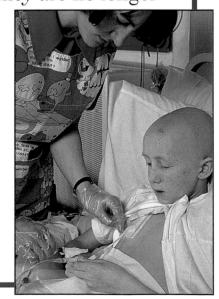

Blood and healing

Cuts and grazes should be washed thoroughly to prevent infection. Press the wound to help stop it bleeding and apply antiseptic to kill germs.

Blood plays a vital role in healing cuts and grazes. If a water pipe in your house bursts, the leak continues until a plumber fixes it, but blood has the amazing ability to clot, or solidify, to plug the leak. Chemical reactions take place in plasma and platelets to cause clotting. Meanwhile white blood cells gather at the wound to fight infection. This is why the area around a cut feels inflamed when you have an injury.

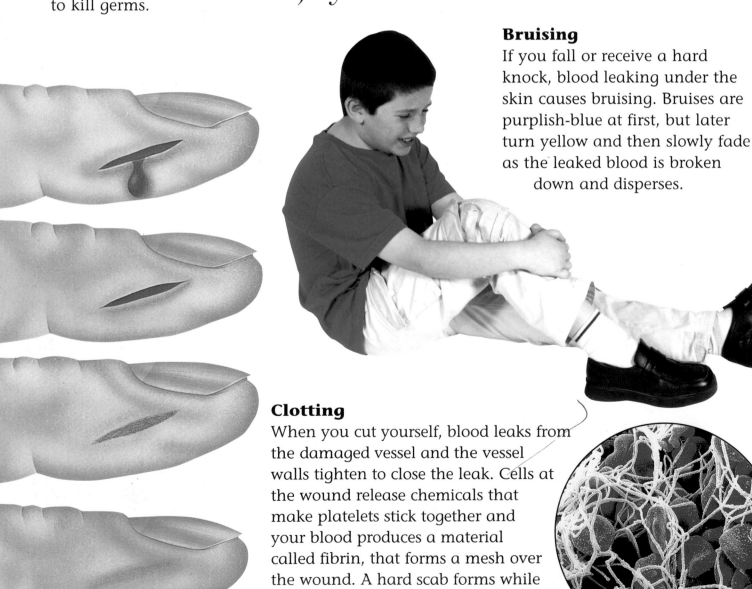

Bruising

If you fall or receive a hard knock, blood leaking under the skin causes bruising. Bruises are purplish-blue at first, but later turn yellow and then slowly fade as the leaked blood is broken down and disperses.

Clotting

When you cut yourself, blood leaks from the damaged vessel and the vessel walls tighten to close the leak. Cells at the wound release chemicals that make platelets stick together and your blood produces a material called fibrin, that forms a mesh over the wound. A hard scab forms while the tissue below heals. When the wound is fully healed, the scab drops off.

Dangerous clots

Clotted blood heals cuts in your skin and damage inside the body. But clotted blood can also be dangerous, if the clot obstructs the flow of blood to a vital organ, such as the heart or brain. A clot in one of the coronary arteries that supply the heart with blood can cause a painful seizure called a heart attack, when part of the heart muscle stops working. 'Clot-busting' drugs can be given to thin the blood of people at risk of heart attacks.

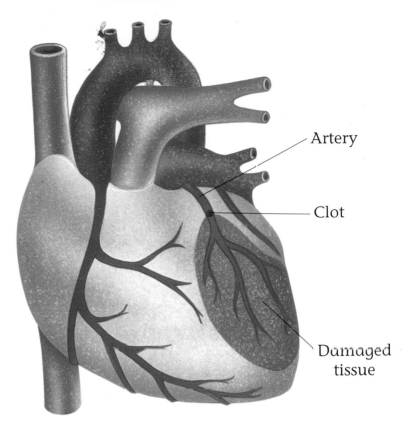

Artery

Clot

Damaged tissue

Tetanus and blood poisoning

Tetanus is a disease that affects the muscles, causing them to spasm (tighten uncontrollably). It is caused by germs that lurk in dirt. Infection is rare but can be caused by cuts from a rusty nail or dirty garden tool for example. Always wash wounds thoroughly to guard against tetanus. You can also be vaccinated against the disease.

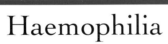

Haemophilia

Haemophilia is an inherited illness that usually affects males, rather than females. People with haemophilia lack a chemical which causes their blood to clot quickly. Bleeding caused by cuts and grazes can still usually be healed by applying a little pressure and a plaster. However, the main problem is any internal bleeding that occurs in joints, muscles and soft tissues. In the past, haemophilia was a serious illness but today, haemophilia can be treated by supplying a patient with the missing chemical.

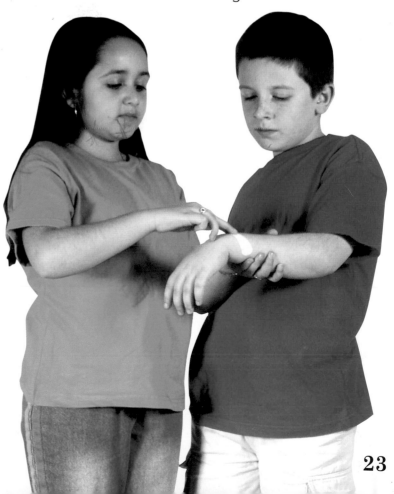

The blood through life

The heart of an unborn baby begins to develop after just three weeks. By five weeks, the embryo's four-chambered heart is pumping blood around the tiny body. At birth, the baby's circulation changes, and continues to change slowly throughout life. As people get older, their circulatory system tends to slow down.

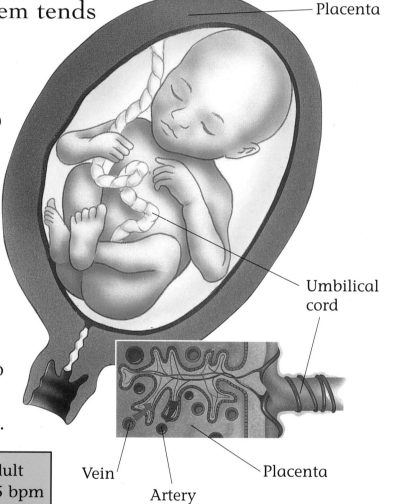

Placenta

Umbilical cord

Placenta

Vein

Artery

Circulation in the womb

An unborn baby cannot breathe or eat to get oxygen and nutrients. Instead, its mother supplies these necessities in her blood. The embryo's circulatory system is linked to a blood-rich organ called the placenta, via the umbilical cord. After birth, the baby's circulation changes, and blood travelling to the placenta is rerouted to receive nutrients and oxygen from the baby's own digestive system and lungs.

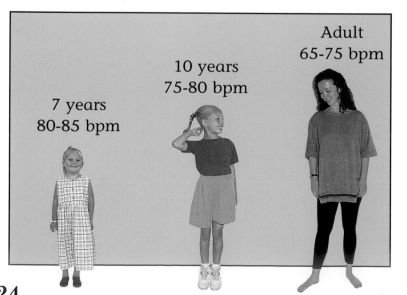

Adult
65-75 bpm

10 years
75-80 bpm

7 years
80-85 bpm

Heart rate through life

Your heart rate gradually changes as you get older. As a new-born baby, your heart rate is very fast. By the age of seven, it drops to about 80-85 beats per minute at rest. By the age of ten, your heart rate averages about 75-80 beats per minute. Adults have an even slower heart rate, averaging 65-75 beats per minute.

Heart repairs

If heart problems develop, doctors can now perform a range of operations to try to repair the damage. If a heart is very badly diseased, it can sometimes be replaced by a new heart given by someone who has recently died. In the future, artificial hearts or even hearts from animals such as pigs may be used in transplant operations.

Blockage

New vein

Surgeons can treat a blocked coronary artery by inserting a blood vessel from the leg to by-pass the block, as shown above. A faulty valve in the heart can be replaced by an artificial valve (shown right).

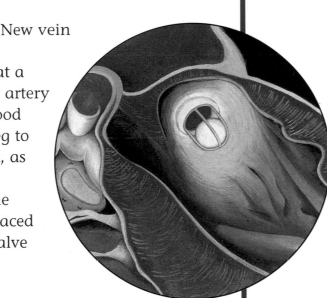

Heart rate is controlled by signals from the brain and the hormone adrenalin. If the heart does not beat steadily, a device called a pacemaker (shown left) can be inserted to regulate the heart beat.

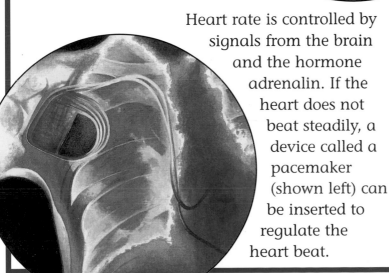

Later in life

As you get older, so the risk of heart problems becomes greater. People over the age of 35 are more likely to suffer a heart attack if they smoke, are overweight, or take little exercise. So, not smoking, eating moderately, and taking regular exercise (above) all help to reduce the risk.

High blood pressure

High blood pressure is a condition that usually affects older people. It can develop as the muscular walls of arteries become less supple and smaller blood vessels get narrower. People with high blood pressure are more likely to suffer a heart attack or stroke. This happens when a blood vessel in the brain bursts or gets blocked, starving surrounding cells of oxygen. Again, cutting down on fatty food, not smoking and exercising regularly all help to lower the risk.

Heart rate and exercise

Your face may get flushed when you exercise, as blood vessels near your skin widen to carry more blood near the surface, allowing heat to escape.

The speed at which your heart beats, and the amount of blood it pumps, depends on how active you are. When you exercise, your muscles need more oxygen, energy and nutrients than when you are at rest. While you are active, your heart pumps faster and your arteries widen to allow blood to flow more freely. Exercise makes you hot. Flushing and sweating are the body's ways of keeping you cool.

Driven by fear

Your heart rate increases when you are scared as well as during exercise. Fear or excitement causes the adrenal glands above your kidneys to release the hormone adrenalin into your blood. This chemical speeds up the heart rate to provide your muscles with the extra energy and oxygen, that might be needed to fight or run away.

Recovery and fitness

The number of times your heart beats every minute while you are resting is called your resting pulse rate. During exercise, your heart pumps faster, but drops back to normal when you stop. The time taken to return to normal is called the recovery rate and is a measure of fitness. To find out your recovery rate, take your pulse while you are resting, exercise for five minutes, and continue to take your pulse every minute until it returns to normal.

200 beats per minute

During exercise, up to four-fifths of your blood flows to your muscles. Your pulse may rise to 200 beats per minute.

Wrap up after exercise

Exercise makes you hot and sweaty, but when you stop, there is a danger of cooling down too quickly. Put on an extra layer of clothing when you finish exercising, to avoid getting too cold. Marathon runners wrap up in shiny foil blankets that trap their body heat after a race. This prevents them from losing their body heat too quickly.

Checking your pulse

The pulse at your wrist is the easiest to measure, using a stop watch (see page 16). You could count the number of beats in 30 seconds and then double it to save time.

Gravity and blood flow

Valves in blood vessels in your limbs and other body parts help your blood to flow 'uphill' against the pull of gravity. Hold one arm in the air for a minute and compare the colour of your hands to see how your blood flows against gravity.

Your heart rate rises slightly after you eat, to 70-90 beats per minute, as blood flows to the digestive system to help break down your food.

50-70 *beats per minute*

When you rest or sleep, your muscles receive about only one-fifth of your blood. Your heart rate drops to 50-70 beats per minute.

70-90 *beats per minute*

Keeping healthy

In developed countries, heart disease is on the increase. Doctors think this is because nowadays many people eat too much fatty food and take too little exercise. It's easy to look after your heart by eating less fat, watching your weight, exercising regularly and not smoking. If you take care in these ways there's every chance your heart will stay strong and healthy.

Exercising too hard or long at first can result in injury. The best way is to start small and build up gradually.

Blood hygiene

If you cut yourself you should wash the wound thoroughly and cover with a dressing to prevent germs from entering your blood. If the wound is deep, it may need to be stitched by a doctor to help it heal properly. If your nose gets a hard knock, blood vessels in the lining of your nose may tear and start to bleed. To stop a nosebleed, hold your head forward and gently squeeze the top of your nose until the blood clots.

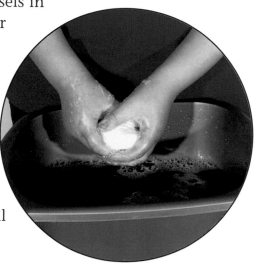

Smoking

As well as causing circulatory problems, smoking also damages the lungs and causes breathing problems. It increases your risk of getting cancer in areas such as the lungs, mouth and throat. Smoking is hard to give up, so it's best never to start.

Healthy heart muscles

Muscles throughout your body get fitter and stronger through exercise. The heart – basically a bag of muscle – is no different. Regular exercise helps keep your heart, bones, joints and muscles trim and supple. Any activity that gets you out and about is a good idea. Remember, you're never too old or too young to get active!

Make it aerobic

Doctors say that doing strenuous exercise lasting 20-30 minutes, three times a week helps to keep your heart, lungs and whole body healthy. Skipping, swimming and dancing are all types of aerobic exercise. Anything that causes your heart and lungs to work harder – but make sure it's fun!

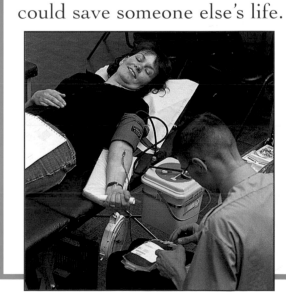

Giving blood

People who lose a lot of blood through injury or during a hospital operation may need to be given a blood transfusion. When you are 18 you can become a blood donor. It only takes a few minutes of your time, but could save someone else's life.

A little bit of what you fancy

A balanced diet nourishes your heart along with the rest of your body. It's best to eat a wide variety of different foods rather than too much of any one thing. A diet that includes at least five portions of fruit and vegetables, and also eggs, nuts, lentils, fish or poultry is perfect. Remember to drink lots of water too.

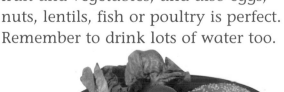

Amazing facts

In a single day, your heart pumps around 10,000 litres of blood. In a few days you'd be able to fill a tanker this size!

Vein

Capillary

Artery

When you are resting, your heart pumps about 5 litres (10 pts) of blood a minute. When you start to exercise it works up to five times as hard, pumping 25 litres (50 pts) per minute.

In an adult, the largest arteries in the body are about 3 cm in diameter. The smallest capillaries are just 0.0001 mm across.

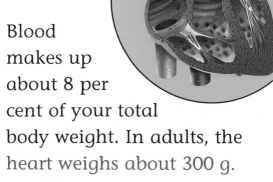

Blood makes up about 8 per cent of your total body weight. In adults, the heart weighs about 300 g.

Your heart beats about 70 times every minute – that's 4,200 times an hour, and 100,800 times a day!

Glossary

Aerobic exercise Any type of exercise that causes the heart and lungs to work harder, pumping oxygen-rich blood to the muscles.

Alveolus [pl. alveoli] A tiny air sac found in the lungs, where oxygen passes into the bloodstream, and carbon dioxide passes into the lungs.

Artery A large blood vessel that carries blood away from the heart.

Atrium One of the two small chambers of the heart.

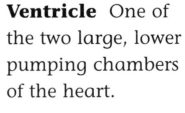

Blood pressure The force that blood exerts on the arteries. Blood pressure varies with strength of the arteries and the force of the heartbeat.

Capillary A tiny blood vessel between an artery and a vein.

Cardiac muscle The special muscle of which the heart is made, that never tires.

Circulatory system The body system that circulates blood around the body, made up of the heart, blood vessels, and the blood itself.

Clot When blood solidifies to seal a wound.

Haemoglobin A red, iron-rich chemical found in red blood cells, that carries oxygen.

Lymph The milky-white fluid that circulates through the body, removing unwanted fluids and fighting infection.

Plasma The liquid part of blood in which blood cells are transported.

Platelet A tiny blood cell which helps blood to clot.

Pulse The rate at which the heart beats to pump blood around the body.

Vaccination The practice of giving the body a substance which primes the immune system to defeat an infection.

Vein A large blood vessel that carries blood to the heart.

Ventricle One of the two large, lower pumping chambers of the heart.

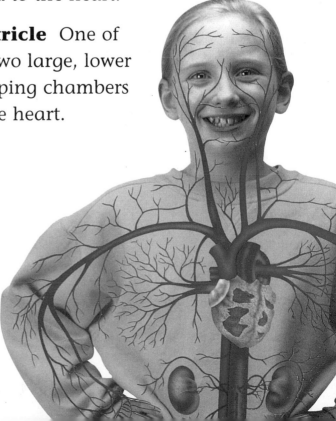

Index

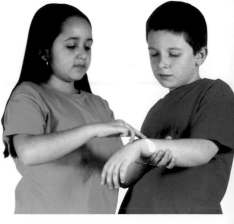

Photo credits

Abbreviations: l-left, r-right, b-bottom, t-top, c-centre, m-middle, ba-background

All photos supplied by PBD except for: Cover, 6bml, 6bmr, 6brl, 10r, 24 all – Roger Vlitos. 4tr, 7bl, 28br – Digital Stock. 5r, 31br – Select Pictures. 6ml, 29tl – Corbis. 8ml – Westminster Hospital/Science Photo Library. 10bmt – Corel. 10bm – Stockbyte. 13tr – Image State. 13br – Alfred Pasieka/Science Photo Library. 17tr – Klaus Guldbrandsen/Science Photo Library. 17br – Digital Vision. 19ml – Science Photo Library. 21br – Simon Fraser/Royal Victoria Infirmary, Newcastle/Science Photo Library. 22br – Susumu Nishinaga/Science Photo Library. 25tr – Photodisc. 27mt – S. Carmona/CORBIS. 29br – Damien Lovegrove/Science Photo Library. 30bl – Corbis Royalty Free.